TEN SHORT PLAYS ABOUT THE CLIMATE CRISIS

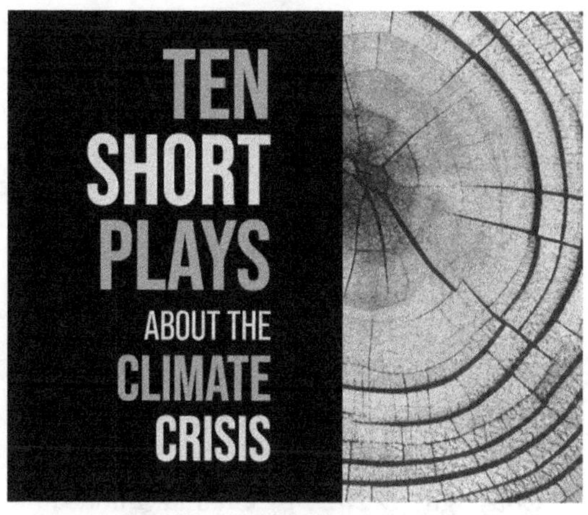

EDITED BY

CHANTAL BILODEAU

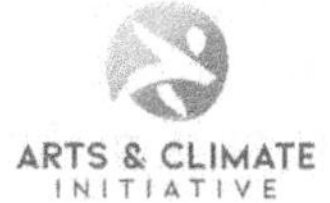

The Centre for Sustainable Practice in the Arts

Published by the Arts & Climate Initiative and the Centre for Sustainable Practice in the Arts
www.artsandclimate.org | www.sustainablepractice.org

First edition

Cover design and typesetting by Causality

Printed in the United States of America

ISBN 979-8-9905439-2-8
ISBN 979-8-9905439-3-5 (ebook)

Ten writers were asked to respond to the prompt "The Time Is Now" for Climate Change Theatre Action 2025 (CCTA), a worldwide festival of short plays about the climate crisis organized by the Arts & Climate Initiative in partnership with the Centre for Sustainable Practice in the Arts. Intentionally open-ended, the prompt can be understood as a call to action or a reminder to stay connected to the present moment, as an ultimatum or the promise of a new beginning. The plays included in this book are the responses. These plays were then paired with forty greatest hits from CCTA's last decade to create the CCTA 2025 collection of fifty plays. For more information about CCTA, visit our website at www.climatechangetheatreaction.com.

CONTENTS

◊ ◊ ◊

SCARY-SCARY

Klae Bainter

This piece kind of emerged from the idea that fear, especially when it comes to climate change, doesn't seem to speak to people in the way it once did. And I don't mean the big, dramatic fear. I'm talking about the little, everyday kind of fear. You know, the kind that's just big enough to give you a gentle push toward doing what's right for the planet. Not the earth-shaking panic, but that quiet, subtle nudge that makes you think twice and choose wisely.

Note

The characters in this play are a crow and a scarecrow. Cast it with whichever flavor of human you wish.

◊ ◊ ◊

SCARECROW is alone in a barren field. CROW rushes in. They are dragging a coin – to scale... a quarter... or some made up currency.

Cautiously walks up on SCARECROW.

CROW: Scarecrow?

Takes a step back.

Scarecrow.

Again.

Scarecrow!

SCARECROW is roused and begins to sit up.

SCARECROW: Go away.

CROW: Please. I don't want to be here either… but get up. Something is coming and you have to be scary, please.

SCARECROW: You, of anyone, should know, little Crow… I'm always scary. Now go away, I say.

CROW: I won't. I know… you're the scariest, I know… but we – I need you to be… *SCARY-scary.*

SCARECROW stirs to life.

SCARECROW: I'm tired, Crow. Leave me alone.

CROW: No. I can't leave. Not until you get up –

SCARECROW jumps up and lets out a terrifying scream at CROW. CROW jumps back.

CROW: Not me! There's a monster! The birds –

SCARECROW: The birds are all gone. Come back in the spring.

CROW: You don't understand. The birds *are* all gone.

SCARECROW: I said that. I have always scared them away.

CROW: Not this time. They're *GONE-gone.*

SCARECROW: No, Crow. I scare away the little *birdies*… like *you, Crows*… those Gulls… and Pigeons. The Buzzards. The Whooping Crane. The Puna Teal. The Blackbirds. The Takahe. Starlings and Finches. The Black-Capped Viero. The Ivory-Billed Woodpecker.

Geese, Curlew, and the Kakapo. The Herons. The California Condor. The Ravens. And then they come back in the spring.

CROW: *I know I know I know.* Listen to me: Everything. Is gone. I can't breathe.

SCARECROW: They come and they go… They come and they go. That's the game we play. Those are the seasons.

CROW: It has *devoured* the seasons! I can't breathe. I can't breathe.

SCARECROW: What has devoured – What are you talking about? Slow, Crow! Slow down!

CROW: The seasons. One by one.

SCARECROW: Winter?

CROW: Bit with its front teeth through cobalt ice.

SCARECROW: It'll return… Summer will shine again and you will see.

CROW: Still steaming when it swallowed it up.

SCARECROW: You are just confused. Everything returns. See, neither season can exist without spring and fall to usher them in.

CROW: Scooped up the pip of spring and the rot of autumn and greedily gobbled them up.

SCARECROW: It can't be. Nothing can do that.

CROW: Yes it can, Scarecrow. The game has gone grave. You have to be scary again. It's a monster!

SCARECROW: The stories of monsters are often worse than the monsters themselves.

CROW: I can't breathe… I can't breathe. You have to be scary.

SCARECROW: What is that you're carrying?

CROW: A coin.

SCARECROW: What's a coin?

CROW: I don't know. They keep appearing. Every time the monster takes something, these are left behind.

SCARECROW: Give it here. Hmm… Could it possibly be food?

CROW: It's flavorless.

SCARECROW: It must be a seed, then.

CROW: It's lifeless.

SCARECROW: Maybe it's a form of protection?

CROW: Soulless.

SCARECROW: You say this monster leaves these in its wake?

CROW: Everywhere. It just continues to take anything and everything without stopping. You need to scare it away!

SCARECROW: It must have a weakness. We could blind the monster. Tell me about the eyes, Crow. Does it blink or bat? Stare, glance, or gaze at the state of things?

CROW: Its eyes are massive and swirling, staring down from the center of dark dangerous clouds. Its tears terrorize everything in its path.

SCARECROW: Well… then we'll have to bind it up! Tell me about its hands. Does it cradle or caress? Does it stroke, tap, pet, or play?

CROW: It doesn't play, Scarecrow. Its hands are bent metal machines that have left great deep gashes in the earth. Massive, muddy sockets where great redwoods once stood.

SCARECROW: We could reason with it. Does this monster speak, Crow? Call? Cry? Hum? Does it ask? Does it question or tell? Does it sing? Does it say? What are its sounds?

CROW: You're not listening to me. There is no reasoning. The sounds the monster makes are a borborygmi of dank droning engines. The pops and cracks of the Earth breaking open and spitting blood. Its sound is the dead silence of stopped rivers and streams. It's the choking quiet of animals that have no more breath with which to chirp, tweet, kuk, bark, growl, hiss, snarl, or scream. No. It does not speak, Scarecrow, because it does not have to.

SCARECROW: Then it really is a monster.

CROW: That's what I've been telling you!

SCARECROW: I cannot help you. I'm sorry.

CROW: What do you mean you cannot help? You have to help! You have to scare it away!

SCARECROW: How can I? Who do you think I am, Crow?

CROW: You are SCARY-scary! You've always scared away the birds. But the birds are gone! You are frightful and intense. The spine-chilling gallybagger. Terrifying and hair-raising might! You are here to make things right, to scare away what needs to be scared away!

SCARECROW: Crow. I'm the curator of a cycle. I chase you off and you come back… You always return. I am here to maintain a balance. To even this field. To protect.

CROW: But the birds are gone. The sun grew hotter and hotter and hotter. It was suffocating… stifling… we couldn't breathe. You have to do something. They couldn't breathe. I couldn't breathe. Do something. I can't breathe… I can't breathe. I can't breathe. I can't breathe.

SCARECROW embraces CROW.

SCARECROW: Slow, Crow. Slow. Slow, Crow. Slow. Slow, Crow. Slow. Slow, Crow. Slow. Why aren't you afraid of me?

CROW: I was afraid of you… You knew where we belonged. The fear you stirred in us kept us moving, growing. It kept us alive.

SCARECROW: The fear was bound by my love for you… for all of you. It fueled our cycle, your journey – and most importantly, it ensured your return. The value of the fields and the vitality of the crops… even *my* existence was made meaningful because of your return. And if they're all gone… if the birds are really gone… then our cycle is over.

CROW: I can't breathe. I can't breathe, Scarecrow. The birds are all gone. You are so scary. You are so scary. I can't breathe. You are… You are… The birds are all gone.

SCARECROW: Shhh. Slow, Crow. Slow. Rest. Rest, Crow. Rest.

SCARECROW puts an arm around CROW. CROW gets close.

CROW's breathing slows.

CROW: If our cycle is complete. Then… you are… You are… You are…

CROW quiets.

SCARECROW: I am obsolete.

Lights.

◊ ◊ ◊

Klae Bainter is the resident playwright and literary manager of convergence continuum in Cleveland, Ohio. His plays use poetic language to examine the grotesque nature of people, their values, and the spaces they hold sacred. His work has been produced in Cleveland, Spokane, Seattle, and Houston. Klae received his MFA in playwriting from Ohio University, and his BA in English Literature & Creative Writing from the University of Washington. He lives with an obnoxious orange cat named Cormac.
klaebainter.wixsite.com/playwright

HERE IN THE LONG NOW

Isla Cowan

This play is inspired by the idea of "chronowashing," which has been proposed and developed by academic Michelle Bastian and represents "a temporal version of greenwashing."[1] While global corporations claim to support long term, planetary-scale thinking and sustainability, they engage in business practices that encourage short-term consumerism and rely on fast-paced production processes – both of which result in significant environmental damage, such as plastic waste and pollution. This play dramatizes these tensions of time and responds with a provocation to the audience.

Characters

SELLERS: To be played by one or more actors.
WORKERS: To be played by one or more actors.
CLOCKMAKER: One actor, but could also be played by more than one actor if appropriate.

Notes

The SELLERS function like a chorus. Lines may be assigned to individuals and smaller groups at the director's discretion to create a cacophony of consumerist voices. These lines should run at a pace and the director may find further opportunities for interruption and overlap.

A slash (/) denotes a point of interruption.
A dash (–) denotes a hesitation or halt in speech, a microbeat.

[1] Bastian, Michelle. "Is Long-Term Thinking a Trap? Chronowashing, Temporal Narcissism, and the Time Machines of Racism." *Environmental Humanities*, 1 July 2024; 16 (2): 403–421. https://doi.org/10.1215/22011919-11150043.

This play features language and terms relating to a UK context. Companies are encouraged to adapt specific elements of the play to suit the location of performance.

The footnotes indicated in the text should be projected or somehow made visible or accessible to the audience to acknowledge the source. If this is not possible, they might be announced by an actor onstage or offstage instead. In this instance, companies are invited to find interesting and provocative ways to stage the relationship between action and citation. Below are the full sources for reference:

Bezos, Jeff. "Welcome to the 10,000 Year Clock Website." *10,000 Year Clock: Sierra Diablo Mountain Range.* https://www.10000yearclock.net/learnmore.html.

Bezos, Jeff. "Amazon's original 1997 letter to shareholders." *About Amazon*, 21 March, 1997. https://www.aboutamazon.com/news/company-news/amazons-original-1997-letter-to-shareholders.

Tweney, Dylan. "How to Make a Clock Run for 10,000 Years." *Wired*, 23 June, 2011. https://web.archive.org/web/20200303100610/https://www.wired.com/2011/06/10000-year-clock/.

◊ ◊ ◊

The SELLERS are scattered across the stage, flaunting their best sale faces. They speak with increasing urgency.

SELLERS: Good morning, Susan. Here's your daily recommendations –

Hello Susan, we found some items we think you might like –

Susan, we thought you might like this –

Customers who viewed this item also viewed –

Customers who viewed *this* item also viewed –

Say thanks with a gift card

What Mum wants, delivered

Share the Joy this Black Friday Week with up to 40% Off

Sale ends in 04 days, 07 hours, 53 minutes

Pick up where you left off

Buy Again

Continue Shopping Deals

We thought you might like this –

Sale ends in 04 days, 05 hours, 47 minutes

Add to Basket?

Buy Again

Get FREE delivery by Wednesday

Or, Fastest One-Day Delivery by tomorrow, 1 p.m.

Order within 06 hours, 07 minutes and choose Fastest Delivery at check-out

Add to Basket?

Sale ends in 02 days, 04 hours, 52 minutes

Order within 04 hours, 27 minutes and choose Fastest Delivery at check-out

Sale ends in 02 days, 03 hours, 19 minutes

Sale ends in 02 days, 03 hours, 01 minute

Add to Basket?

A clock bell chimes.
Somewhere else, the CLOCKMAKER. He speaks to the audience.

CLOCKMAKER: Welcome to the 10,000 Year Clock! Otherwise known as the Clock of the Long Now.

"We are building a 10,000 Year Clock. It's a special Clock, designed to be a symbol, an icon for long-term thinking."[2]

"It's of monumental scale inside a mountain in West Texas."[3]

"… a Clock that ticks once a year, where the century hand advances once every 100 years, and the cuckoo comes out on the millennium. The vision was, and still is, to build a Clock that will keep time for the next 10,000 years."[4]

"As I see it, humans are now technologically advanced enough that we can create not only extraordinary wonders but also civilization-scale problems."[5]

---

[2] Jeff Bezos in "Welcome to the 10,000 Year Clock Website." *10,000 Year Clock: Sierra Diablo Mountain Range.*
[3] Jeff Bezos in "Welcome to the 10,000 Year Clock Website." *10,000 Year Clock: Sierra Diablo Mountain Range.*
[4] Jeff Bezos in "Welcome to the 10,000 Year Clock Website." *10,000 Year Clock: Sierra Diablo Mountain Range.*
[5] Jeff Bezos in "Welcome to the 10,000 Year Clock Website." *10,000 Year Clock: Sierra Diablo Mountain Range.*

"We're likely to need more long-term thinking."[6]

A clock bell chimes.
The SELLERS speak with more pace and pressure now.

SELLERS: Hi Susan. We noticed that you added one or more items to your Shopping Basket, but didn't continue to checkout

Unless you've already done so, simply visit your Shopping Basket when you're ready to complete your order

Simply visit your Shopping Basket when you're ready

It's that simple, Susan

Simply visit your Shopping Basket when you're ready to complete your order

Complete your order

Complete your order, Susan

Continue Shopping Deals

Top Offers

Frequently bought together –

Inspired by your browsing history –

Other people are looking at this

Other people want this

[6] Jeff Bezos in "Welcome to the 10,000 Year Clock Website." *10,000 Year Clock: Sierra Diablo Mountain Range.*

What if they take it and you don't get it?

What if they take it now?

Don't you want it, Susan?

Don't you want it now?

Quick, fast, before they get it first!

Only 3 left in stock

Selling Fast!

Get FREE delivery by Friday, or Fastest One-Day Delivery by tomorrow, 1 p.m. Add to Basket?

Well, don't you want it *now*, Susan?

Don't you *need* it now?

This plastic piece of crap that won't last the week – but you can always buy another. Just throw it in the trash and buy another one after. Because who has to know? Who has to care? Who is it hurting?

Because it'll do the trick for now

It'll make you feel good for now

Complete for now

Complete your order now

The SELLERS get faster and more frantic, overlapping.

Only 2 left in stock

Tomorrow, 1 p.m.

Order within 05 hours, 31 minutes and choose Fastest Delivery at check-out

Tomorrow, 1 p.m.

Sale ends in 01 day, 16 hours, 32 minutes

Only 1 left in stock!

Add to Basket?

Sale ends in /

Add to Basket?

Tomorrow, 1 p.m.

Add to Basket?

Buy Now?

Buy /

A clock bell chimes.

CLOCKMAKER: "My opinion is that human attention spans haven't changed much over time. We've always been a fairly short-sighted species."[7]

SELLERS: Sale ends in 09 hours, 26 minutes

[7] Jeff Bezos, as quoted in Dylan Tweney's "How to Make a Clock Run for 10,000 Years." *Wired*, 23 June, 2011.

CLOCKMAKER: "But while our attention spans are staying roughly constant /"[8]

SELLERS: Sale ends in 05 hours, 13 minutes

CLOCKMAKER: "our problems are becoming much bigger /"[9]

SELLERS: Sale ends in 01 hour, 01 minute

CLOCKMAKER: "because of our past successes as a species. /"[10]

SELLERS: Add to basket?

CLOCKMAKER: "Our tools /"[11]

SELLERS: Buy Now!

CLOCKMAKER: "our technologies /"[12]

SELLERS: Selling Fast!

CLOCKMAKER: "now require us to / step it up, and /"[13]

SELLERS: Sale ends in / 05 hours, 13 minutes

CLOCKMAKER: "have a longer attention span."[14]

---

[8] Jeff Bezos, as quoted in Dylan Tweney's "How to Make a Clock Run for 10,000 Years." *Wired*, 23 June, 2011.
[9] Jeff Bezos, as quoted in Dylan Tweney's "How to Make a Clock Run for 10,000 Years." *Wired*, 23 June, 2011.
[10] Jeff Bezos as quoted in Dylan Tweney's "How to Make a Clock Run for 10,000 Years." *Wired*, 23 June, 2011.
[11] Jeff Bezos as quoted in Dylan Tweney's "How to Make a Clock Run for 10,000 Years." *Wired*, 23 June, 2011.
[12] Jeff Bezos as quoted in Dylan Tweney's "How to Make a Clock Run for 10,000 Years." *Wired*, 23 June, 2011.
[13] Jeff Bezos as quoted in Dylan Tweney's "How to Make a Clock Run for 10,000 Years." *Wired*, 23 June, 2011.
[14] Jeff Bezos as quoted in Dylan Tweney's "How to Make a Clock Run for 10,000 Years." *Wired*, 23 June, 2011.

SELLERS: Sale ends in /

CLOCKMAKER: Like I've always said /

SELLERS: Buy Now!

CLOCKMAKER: "it's all about /"

SELLERS: BUY NOW!

CLOCKMAKER: "the Long Term."[15]

SELLERS: NOW!

A clock bell starts ringing.

Workers in a warehouse.

A production line.

The Workers package plastic items into cardboard boxes. They pass them along, tape them up, pass them along, slap an address sticker on them, pass them along –

At the end of the production line, the final worker opens the boxes and scatters all the plastic, the packaging, and waste all over the stage.

This is repeated until the stage is covered in waste.

Meanwhile, the other workers pack faster and faster to keep up. They become frantic, breathless.

The clock bell rings louder and louder.

[15] Jeff Bezos, "Amazon's original 1997 letter to shareholders," *About Amazon*, 21 March 1997.

CLOCKMAKER, *triumphant*: "In the year 4,000, you'll go see this clock and you'll wonder: Why on Earth did they build this?"[16]

A worker collapses.

◊ ◊ ◊

Isla Cowan is an award-winning playwright, performer, and director, from Scotland. Isla specializes in making ecofeminist theatre and is committed to exploring issues of class, gender, and ecology in her work. In 2024, Isla was Resident Writer at the Tron Theatre, Glasgow, and Playwright in Residence (IASH) at The Traverse Theatre, Edinburgh. Recent plays include: *Alright Sunshine* (Tron Theatre), *To Save the Sea* (Sleeping Warrior), *She Wolf* (Assembly Roxy: Assembly ART Award, Alpine Fellowship Theatre Prize, Filipa Bragança Nominee), *To the Bone* (Pitlochry Festival Theatre), *And… And… And…* (Strange Town Touring Company), and *Daphne, or Hellfire* (Pleasance).
www.islacowan.com

[16] Jeff Bezos as quoted in Dylan Tweney's "How to Make a Clock Run for 10,000 Years." *Wired*, 23 June 2011.

THE LAUNCH

Angie Farrow

The concept of the green city has long inspired me. When I wrote *The Launch*, it was a way of exploring how humans might coexist with nature in an urban setting. I created a trio of activists who set up a greening project in an urban enclave. Their accomplishments seem to match their idealism, but at the high point of their success, they have to look back and consider the real cost of their endeavors. The play asks: "How do we find a balance between our need to make a difference and our psychological well-being?"

Characters

LUCAS (30s): The scientist.
GEORGIE (30s): The entrepreneur.
STU (30s): The visionary.

◊ ◊ ◊

We are in the lobby of City Hall. GEORGIE and STU wear expensive suits. They speak directly to audience members as if they were press reporters.

STU, *responding to reporter*: Can you repeat the question? Well, yes, it was Georgie here who came up with the idea. We were having a few beers one night in her yurt –

GEORGIE, *laughing*: More than a few!

STU: – and she's like: "Let's green the city." We thought she was crazy back then.

GEORGIE: Plastered, more like!

STU: In fact, she's still crazy...

GEORGIE: Hey!

STU: But look what's happened ten years later! "The Green Capital of the Year!"

GEORGIE: Stu loves to brag!

STU, *responding to a question*: Sorry? No, no, I'm just the nerd of the outfit, the boring scientist.

GEORGIE: The brains!

STU: Georgie's the one with the business savvy.

An announcement echoes over the loudspeaker: "This is your five-minute call."

GEORGIE, *to STU*: Where the hell is he?

STU, *to reporters*: We're expecting our other teammate, Lucas. He's our ideas man. We call him "Eco-Einstein."

GEORGIE, *to reporters, moving away with her mobile*: Excuse me!

STU: In a loving way!

GEORGIE speaks into her mobile.

GEORGIE: Lucas! Will you pick up? And for the fiftieth time – two thousand people are out in the square waiting for us to start the launch. You've got four minutes to get here or you're a dead man. *(to reporters)* Sorry about that!

STU, *to reporters*: We'll take a question from the woman at the back. *(responding to question)* Yes, it's easy just to focus on the glamour projects...

GEORGIE: ... the stuff the mayor loves to crow about.

STU : Oh, you know... the vertical farms...

GEORGIE: ... the community gardens...

STU: ... the edible rooftops!

GEORGIE: Stu got a shitload of volunteers to build a tiny forest where the central car park used to be.

STU: Have you seen the hydroponic farm? That was Lucas's baby. Truly amazing!

GEORGIE: It all sounds glamorous, but getting some of it started was sheer slog!

STU, *to GEORGIE*: So where is Lucas?

GEORGIE, *to STU*: I told you. No one's seen him for two days.

STU, *to GEORGIE*: Does he know about...?

GEORGIE, *to STU*: Of course, he knows. But if he's pulling one of his stupid stunts, I'll –

STU, *to GEORGIE*: He's been stressed!

GEORGIE, *to STU*: We've all been stressed, Stu.

STU, *to reporters, responding to a question*: Of *course*, there's greenwashing. Companies pretend they care when all they want are the favorable optics.

GEORGIE: We've made a lot of mistakes.

STU: But you can't do this work without all the dealmaking.

GEORGIE: You just have to be careful who you shake hands with.

STU: Improving public transport was a biggie. High-risk! Capital-intensive!

GEORGIE: And we needed massive investments in renewable energy.

STU: At first, they said we were taking people back to the dark ages.

GEORGIE: But as we kept bleating over and over...

STU/GEORGIE: "We're nudging people back to nature."

> *There is the sound of salsa music. LUCAS enters dancing. He is wearing a suit, but no shoes.*

GEORGIE, *to LUCAS*: Lucas! What the hell?

STU, *to LUCAS, through his teeth*: This had better not be another of your crazy –

GEORGIE: Where have you been?

LUCAS: I've been practicing my salsa routine!

STU: What?

LUCAS, *demonstrating his dance*: What do you think?

STU, *to reporters*: Oh, take no notice! Lucas is just a bit –

An announcement echoes over the loudspeaker: "This is your three-minute call."

STU: You can at least put your shoes on.

GEORGIE: And turn the damn music off.

LUCAS turns the music down. He begins to remove his tie.

LUCAS, *to reporters*: Mulberry silk! None of your cheap shit!

GEORGIE: What are you doing?

LUCAS, *to reporters*: You know how much these suits cost? *(beat)* Not even close! We're talking four figures here. *(taking off his jacket)* One of the gifts from our gracious sponsors.

STU: Have you been drinking?

LUCAS: Possibly! We started out as innocent tree huggers, you know. Down on our luck! Struggling to pay the rent.

GEORGIE: Where are you going with this?

LUCAS: Until we started getting ahead of ourselves. Cosying up to all those industry players. Sweet talking all those fat wallets!

STU: You're out of line, Lucas!

LUCAS: And oh, the honors! The celebrity! *(removing his shirt)* Did you know Georgie made the cover of the *Woman's Weekly*? "How I Managed my Stress at the High End."

GEORGIE: Stop this!

LUCAS: Stu here is the new guru at international business summits. "Eco-Leadership in a Changing Climate!" Eat your heart out, Simon Sinek.

GEORGIE: You need to stop now!

LUCAS, *removing his trousers*: We can't go anywhere without being seen to be seen. Gala openings! TV interviews! We've even got our own fan club. Georgie's shaping up to be the city's Greenie Goddess.

STU, *trying to leave*: Come on, Georgie.

LUCAS: Only, before you go, I'm just wondering: What changed? Is this what we meant? Or did we used to be a bit less... fancy? A bit more real?

STU: Who cares about how real we are if we got the job done?

LUCAS: And what was the cost?

GEORGIE: We got people working together. Old people. Lonely people. We've made beautiful spaces. What's got into you?

LUCAS: Only, I haven't talked to my sick mum for months. And did you know? Janie just threw me out of the house. Said I wasn't the man she married. I was going to tell you but –

GEORGIE: I'm sorry!

LUCAS: – you were always too busy!

STU: Did you just come here to ruin everything?

LUCAS: No!

STU: Well, you're making a bloody good job of it!

LUCAS falls silent.

GEORGIE: We're late already!

LUCAS: I came because I don't want us turning into the people we used to hate. I used to believe what we were saying. I loved wearing frayed old tee shirts and not bothering to shave! Having time to dance! Remember the dancing? Look at us! Cashmere suits! Strutting our stuff like we own the place! I don't even recognize us.

An announcement echoes over the loudspeaker: "Final call for the Dream Team. This is your final call."

STU: There's a cost to everything. Every damn thing, Lucas. But we've all been roughed up by this. All of us! Rearranged! That doesn't have to stop us, does it?

GEORGIE: What did you say back in the day when we got into strife? Let's reset!

STU: Come on man, we need you.

GEORGIE: They're expecting three people on that podium.

STU, *handing him his clothes*: Are you coming?

STU and GEORGIE leave. LUCAS remains holding his clothes. Salsa music rises in volume. The lights fade.

◊ ◊ ◊

Angie Farrow ONZM is Professor Emerita at Massey University, New Zealand. She has won over twenty international and national prizes and awards for her plays. Her short plays have featured in festivals in India, Malaysia, Canada, Australia, the UK, the US, and Singapore. Angie has had six volumes of her plays published in Australia and New Zealand, including *Falling and Other Short Plays*, featuring sixteen of her short works. Her most recent plays have focused on issues around climate change and are included in her most recent publication, *Disobedience and Other Climate Change Plays*.

SPACE CAT

Lewis Hetherington

This play is about an astronaut who is sent into deep space to find a new planet for humans to live on, and a cat who sits at home wondering where he's gone. I wanted to write about the barrenness of space in comparison to this extremely beautiful planet we've been given. I wanted to ask why we are being sold this vision of space colonization and who will actually benefit from it.

I'd like to thank Nicole Cooper, Michael Guest, and Rosalind Sydney for their wonderful insight and input as I was developing the play.

Note

Can be played by any two people. Please feel free to change pronouns to match those used by the performers. If you would like to use a different name than Ralf for the cat, then I suggest Jessie.

1.

RALF: He's coming back. He always comes back.
I mean, I'm fine. I'm not worried. And I like my own space, everyone knows that.
Padding about. Watching the world go by. But he's just. Well, I want to know that he's ok.

AJ: This is it! I'm on the edge of everything. Like the first ever sailor with the first ever boat looking out to sea back in, well, whenever that would have been.

I didn't ever think I would be important. And I didn't mind. But when this came up, it spoke to something inside me. Something vast. Something important.

RALF: He likes to fall asleep in the sunshine. He likes to eat his breakfast slowly whilst listening to the birds. What if there aren't birds where he is? What if he doesn't have his special mug for coffee?

AJ: Leaving the Earth's atmosphere felt like something was tearing inside of me. But they said that would happen. They prepared us for everything. Training was hard but everyone was really nice. And it's software doing most of the work. And the people back down on the ground.

It's not just me. There's loads of us. All in separate pods. Normal people given this chance. Drifting off into the great beyond.

It doesn't matter who finds something. Obviously, it would be nice if it was me. But that's not what's important.

RALF: Look, I miss him ok? I do. I mean, I know everyone says cats are loners and they don't care about anyone, and maybe that's true for some cats but not me, actually. So yeah. I do miss him. I want him to come home.

2.

AJ: 264 days now. Not that days mean anything in space. It's like a corridor with no windows, doors, or end. So that's why we have to keep this Well-Being Log. There's all these mental and physical exercises to keep us right. There is a dot on a screen and it zips about and you have to tap it to catch it. It makes this little sound.

beep beep!

It's really satisfying.

beep beep!

Oh and if you thought airplane food was bad, you should try spaceship food! What else?

I keep thinking about seeing Earth. I know I said before but just seeing it there, blue and green, a glowing ball of life spinning in space. It was weeks ago, but if I close my eyes I can still just about see it.

3.

RALF: Doors open and close, but it's never him. Someone else lives here now. She smells like him, but she's sort of annoying. And she snores. We keep to ourselves. She does buy me little treats sometimes. I keep looking out for him. He's coming back.

AJ: There's nothing here.
Just dust and nothing.
It's not like I thought I'd stumble across a new home planet straight away but...

Did you see that film, *Avengers: Infinity War?* Space in that is all green and purple and swirling. I mean, I knew it wouldn't be like that but...

I keep thinking about my cat. Ralf. I bet he hasn't even noticed I've gone! Silly really. My sister moved in. They'll be fine.

454 days now.

Onwards for humanity! That's one of the affirmations they gave us.

RALF: What is taking so long? What is he doing? What's more important than being here?

AJ: I sent a message to the company. I said: If we do find a new planet, can my cat come? They said no.

RALF: I look for him all the time. I go out on the balcony and look for his bouncy walk below.

AJ: 689 days.

Ralf is maybe dead by now. In cat years, he would be, I don't know, but really old.

That tear inside me, it feels bigger. The machines say I'm fine. They need our bodies to respond to samples from the planets. They keep blood moving to keep my flesh alive to see if it gets poisoned.

I hope Ralf will be ok at the end. I don't know what it's like for a cat at the end.

4.

RALF: I'm so tired now. My bones are achy and it feels like I'm sinking. I just want to see him again. Was my breath always this thin? He'll come back now, won't he? He'll come back and put his hand on my tummy.

What was that? No. Nothing. It's all just shapes and light now. I can't see very much. But I'll know him. His voice, his smell, his hand on my tummy.

He needs to hurry up! I don't think there's long now. I want to hear his funny little noise that he does to get my attention. He goes:

AJ: *meow meow meow*

RALF: And I run to him! Not now. I can't run to him anymore. I'm sinking. I'm sinking away to somewhere else. And then, I'm gone.

AJ: *meow meow meow*

Obviously, it won't work to bring him out here. But it's nice because for a split second, I get this little lift, as though he might appear.

meow meow meow

I used to sit on my balcony in the sun. Ralf would sit in my lap. We'd fall asleep as I was stroking the soft fur of his underbelly.

There was a little wooden box and I grew rosemary. I don't remember how it smelt but I remember I liked it. I'd pick a bit and Ralf would nibble it.

We'd watch the birds. The clouds would drift and sometimes the sky was pink and purple as the sun was setting.

Maybe when he died, his soul floated out into space and he is drifting towards me. Maybe I'll see him. Whiskers glowing and eyes alive. He'll drift up to me and his ghost white paws will tap gently at my face saying, come on, get up. And then maybe his gentle ghost body will weave between my legs before he drifts onwards to cat heaven.

But probably not.

Day 904.

I wonder if everyone is dead.

Maybe Earth is just another planet of poisonous gas and dust now, like all these ones.

Maybe there has been some brilliant and clever technical solution, which just swept in and solved everything.

Oh, but that's what this is meant to be. Maybe I'll find something and save everyone.

I just want to see my cat.

5.

AJ: 3,467 days

I really

beep beep!

sorry my brain is flooded

and my eyeballs are swollen

I really

what was the smell it was

muscles like a popped balloon

old plastic bags

atrophied, they told us this would happen
but they weren't

there's no planet, is there? not for someone like me

meow meow meow

I really did have...

Ralf

I was a normal human, you know, and I thought that was nothing but it was not, it was not nothing

beep beep

the machines make it so we can't die. For the mission

maybe if I get to the edge of the universe, then I will die and have a moment of euphoria

breath in my lungs
a cat in my lap
the scent of rosemary in the air

I really did have it all, didn't I? I had it all. And then

◊ ◊ ◊

Lewis Hetherington is an award-winning playwright, whose work is rooted in storytelling and play. He often works in community contexts and is passionate about using creativity to empower people to find connection and agency. He has created work for National Theatre of Scotland, Citizens Theatre, Platform National Youth Theatre, Traverse Theatre, Edinburgh International Festival, and Historic Scotland, among others. His work has travelled to China, Canada, Saudi Arabia, Australia, US, Japan, and across all of Scotland, where he lives.
www.lewishetherington.com

LANDFORMS

Andrea Ling

I was drawn to explore the tension between time running out and the land that holds it, to capture the anxiety of a world on the brink. It is an honest reckoning with our inaction, the complexity. It is a search for why, despite knowing the urgency of the climate crisis, real change remains unidentifiable.

Notes

The space is a rapid shifting constellation – forming, flashing, vanishing, and reappearing. Time and the text's rhythm move at speed. A slash (/) indicates the next line is delivered immediately. Capitalization of a word indicates a stress. The play invites boldness: to explore movement, light, transitions, sound. Ideally, there is no multi-rolling. Pronouns can be changed.

◊ ◊ ◊

BEST FRIEND: He's not Technically missed valentines, not yet

SHE, *to audience*: It's friday, 11 a.m., I should be working

BEST FRIEND: He's into cars, flash ones, I don't understand, but Today he's gone track racing and spent eight hundred pounds, Eight Hundred Quid, Eight Hundred, on One day to race his Car on a Track

SHE, *to audience*: For our international viewers, that's over a thousand dollars, or fifteen thousandths of a milli-bitcoin. This feels already hopeless…

BEST FRIEND: Hello?

SHE: Sorry, I'm in shock

BEST FRIEND: And for valentines, he's bringing Fucking Takeaway. I don't get it because he believes climate change is real, and he Wants to do his part and knows /

SHE: That you work as a sustainability consultant?

BEST FRIEND: Yes, and that I choose Not to have a car for the environment. It doesn't seem to compute in his stupid brain this oxymoron

SHE: I'm not sure that's how / oxymoron

BEST FRIEND: But I'm falling in love

SHE: Oh shit

PARTNER: Shit? You've been doomscrolling for / about

SHE: Not doomscrolling, ethical consumer-based research… I'm having a crisis of jumpers

PARTNER: Oh no!

SHE: Keep your sarcasm, this is genuinely hard, ethics versus wants, needs, money and now I'm in a wormhole of fabric doom, greenwashing, and intricate clothing manufacturing processes… All to justify that I've seen a jumper and I Really want it

PARTNER: Fuck, it's three hundred quid. And the other?

SHE, *to the audience*: This is my partner by the way. *(to PARTNER)* Way cheaper, nice, wool but with rayon….

PARTNER: Can't you fix what / you have?

SHE: I don't have time to Fucking fix them!

Partner: But time to be on your phone shopping?

SHE: Ohhh I could / just

PARTNER: Kiss this sexy face?… Also, you could close your mouth and not look angry, that would help…

SHE: You have such a punchable face right now…

PARTNER: How about you kiss this punchable face! *(pulls a horrid facial expression)*

SHE: No! *(runs away from kiss, turns and…)* Hey! You can't throw out new flooring

"RECYCLER:" Watch me

SHE, *to audience*: Recycling center, Sunday, time really flies. *(to "RECYCLER")* That's Brand New, not even opened, still wrapped in plastic

"RECYCLER:" No one wants flooring that only covers a doormat. Now, Fuck Off

SHE: Imagine: Everything that we have Ever thrown away arrives back in our home, a mountain of our personal waste reaching the tops of ceilings, every crevice. Would we all suffocate in our own waste?

"RECYCLER:" Fucking Psycho!

SHE: Ouch

"RECYCLER," *walking away*: You're just the same, getting rid of unwanted things. Just playing the woke bitch!

SHE: It all just makes me sick / too!

COUPLE 1: What makes you sick?

We jumped to a dinner party.

SHE: The convenience of throwing away / the politicization of being aware, if it's Recycled, it's ok…

PARTNER: Babe you're interrupting /

COUPLE 2: No, it's probably connected in some way…

SHE: I don't remember getting here

Pause.

COUPLE 2: I'll get you a glass of water

COUPLE 1: You know, I watched a documentary on recycling showing how a lot went to landfills in Turkey

COUPLE 2: Darling, not now

COUPLE 1: It's on topic and now, I'm afraid to say, I refuse to recycle, it's pointless

SHE: How the Fuck are we suppose to Tackle Anything if you just Wipe Your Hands Clean!

PARTNER: Sit down, babe

SHE: Am I standing?

ACTIVIST 1: Sit down! Stand up!

ACTIVISTS 1, 2, 3: No More Coal, No More Oil, Keep Your Carbon In The Soil!

SHE: I can't handle this. I might throw up

ACTIVIST 1: We are living in an emergency!

SHE: I feel it, I'm with you, and I'm trying… I do want to say thank you, but I do question: Is this still working? Promises have been broken, nothing has changed

ACTIVIST 2: We need stronger civil disobedience, we need to apply this pressure

SHE: Yet civil disobedience has created this subculture of Fascist Loving Carbon Monsters

ACTIVIST 3: We're not just facing climate change, we're now facing Social Collapse followed by effective Extinction

She vomits.

PARTNER: It's not pregnancy?

SHE: Oh god. Please, weren't we just at a protest? Tell me you were with me

PARTNER: Babe, you're jumping from one subject to the next. This is important, we were talking about children

SHE: No, no, no… With lack of money, rising costs, wars, drought, floods, fires, depression, social injustice, we can't have children

PARTNER: It is confusing, you're Confusing me. It's hard to know where you are, you keep switching

SHE: All this, this Feeling, this… pressure, this All Encompassing Decisions on Every Aspect, it's all connected to, to…

PARTNER: Calm, breathe, remember / I love you

SHE: I can't stay here

A firm arriving to a lavish meeting room.

SHE: Do humans just need to be told what to do? I'm scared to say this but maybe we need a good, kind, liberal dictatorship, can that exist?

DICTATOR, *laughing*: If you truly grow up in a culture of democracy, you must expect to deal with, even welcome, polar viewpoints, and serve many different types of needs, some which you vehemently disagree with. As a dictator, you need the courage to destroy multiple viewpoints. Would you have the strength?

Abrupt arrival.

SHE: Babe, let's buy a piece of land, a quiet space, off-grid, live off the land, have kids… Would the climate last long enough?

PARTNER: You're fading from me

SHE: We could run away or… if we don't have children… we won't have to worry

PARTNER: You're letting your anxiety choose for you

SHE: Why not?

PARTNER: Please, don't leave this time

SHE: I can't seem to control it

CEO: There is hope. With Beyond Earth, we cover everything that happens in space, such as debris removal of old satellites, and with Space Solar, we are trying to build a solar power station in space, which beams the power back to Earth through microwaves. All sci-fi sounding but genuinely happening right now

SHE: We don't hear about it

CEO: Think clean energy 24/7, that's our future

SHE: I can't shake that it's too good to be true. Where is the balance?

CEO: You don't tell people to turn off their lights, you build them a better light bulb

SHE: This is what got us here in the first place! Can we trust those who have the power? Who holds the power?

PRESIDENT: The mandate

CEO: Stop complaining and do something

SHE: I am, I'm asking questions

FAR RIGHT: Woke culture, go paint a Fucking Painting

PARTNER: I'm always right here

ANCESTOR: Been always here

SHE: Art is talking about it now, this play

FAR RIGHT: Play?

PARTNER: What the fuck are you on about?

SHE: I'm losing my mind but I think I need to, with it things are connecting I promise

PARTNER: We need professional help, babe, you're relapsing

SHE: No no no, listen, I had a dream I'm sat across an open arid landscape of mountains and dust, I'm in traditional dress, kneeling, with my mother and grandmother on either side of me, and behind me a lineage of women, my ancestors, and women in front of me, all connected. It was like calling a spirit, calling mine own…

A large breath and moment.

SHE, *to audience*: I'm in a rocky expanse. It's so silent.

ANCESTOR: Come sit.

SHE, *to audience*: An ancestor.

ANCESTOR: Feel the rock. Trace your fingers.

SHE, *to audience*: I do.

ANCESTOR: You feel it? A beginning, ending, and its cycle?

She nods.

ANCESTOR: The land is a tapestry of time, each compression an epoch, the trials and tribulations visibly written into our rocks. Deep time, a time not bound by human concepts, not the fleetingness of human life, there is not one, but a collection of, a vessel of the many.

SHE: These fragments…

ANCESTOR: Create our landforms.

SHE: It's… this touch… there's no word for it?

Sound of the wind caressing a mountain.

So calm. I think I shall wait a while here.

ANCESTOR: He's waiting for you.

SHE: I can't. I'm scared to go back, scared of running out of time.

ANCESTOR: Do you think the Earth moves by human time? Our ancestors knew that land and time are not separate. All things Earth, spirits, time – it is not past or future, it simply is as one. Some whisper it as Pacha, Ceiba, Ubuntu, Rta, Sanquofa, Vā, Tengri.

Whispers repeat softly into wind and land.

SHE: Thank you.

ANCESTOR: Always.

A steady breath.

SHE: I'm back. *(waits)* Thought you would be here, our favorite place, the smell, the cold wet air.

I'm sorry.

PARTNER: You scared me.

SHE: I know, yes. I scared myself. But I needed to see from a far distance, what it all was.

PARTNER: And so you left.

SHE: I had to search, will keep searching beyond one lifetime, beyond maybe human existence, but, in a less manic way. I'm sorry. Time made me feel so anxious, guilty, it just escapes you.

PARTNER: I want to understand.

SHE: You see this rock, the landform's surface, that's us. *(traces with fingers)*

Partner laughs.

PARTNER: Hold my hand. I have hope and I will hold your hand through all of it, through the storms, fears, anxiety, through time. I'll hold your hand on this landform that is home.

Sound of nature, time, and landforms envelop.

◊ ◊ ◊

Andrea Ling is an interdisciplinary artist: a director, writer, dramaturg, visual artist, and educator working within theatre and installation. She is Bolivian-British-Chinese and lives in Glasgow. Andrea is currently the Director Fellow at National Theatre of Scotland. She founded the arts company Pacha People, which creates art *for*, and *with*, underrepresented communities to incite social change. In 2020, Andrea won the Jerwood Live Work Award and in 2023, she was awarded the Genesis Future Directors Award. www.andrealing.com and www.pachapeople.com

EAT THE RICH

Tira Palmquist

Anger (or despair) is a rational response to watching the impacts of climate change. While none of us are blameless, the wealthy pollute the most, and the impacts are felt disproportionately on those who can least afford it. This is a play about channeling anger.

Characters

KAI: An orca. The matriarch and consensus-builder.
DELMAR: Also an orca. The rule-follower.
STEVE: You guessed it: an orca. The rebel. Wearing a t-shirt that says "EAT THE RICH."

Setting

In the Atlantic Ocean.

Time

Now.

Note

The actors, despite what the names suggest, can be cast as you will. It's 2025. Be brave.

◊ ◊ ◊

Lights up on a heated negotiation between orcas from the same pod.

DELMAR: Ramming boats is just stupid! More stupid than those salmon you were wearing as hats!

STEVE: You wish you could carry off a salmon hat, Delmar.

KAI: Steve, listen: Delmar is just upset about all the bad press.

STEVE: Bad press? Kai, come on.

DELMAR, *pulling out a phone and reading headlines*: "Off Spain's Coast, Orcas Ram Sailboats" –

STEVE: Sailboats, sure. No one should be ramming sailboats.

DELMAR, *reading*: "Yacht Sinks After Latest Incident Involving Orcas" –

STEVE: Delmar, *loads* of orcas ram yachts.

DELMAR, *reading*: "Killer Whales Ramming Boats May Be Bored" –

STEVE: Wait – what? That's a damn lie!

KAI: So, you're not ramming boats?

STEVE: Oh, I definitely am. But I'm not *bored*.

KAI: That makes it ok?

STEVE: What can I say? Yes, I've rammed some yachts! Can you blame me?

KAI: Yes! And that's Delmar's point: It's bad enough that we continue to get smeared by terms like "wolves of the seas" or "killer whales" or "murder pandas" –

STEVE: "Murder pandas?" That's kinda cool!

DELMAR: It's not cool, Steve! And you have to stop sinking small watercraft!

STEVE: Delmar! Of course! Obviously! *(seeing DELMAR's confused look)* I mean – I'm not ramming small watercraft. I've moved on. Bigger fish and all that.

KAI: Oh no...

STEVE: Oh yes, Kai. Do you know who the biggest polluters in the North Sea are?

KAI: The... petroleum industry?

STEVE: Probably, yes, that. But – no! Cruise ships!

DELMAR: Cruise ships are too big! You can't sink a cruise ship!

STEVE: Well, not with that attitude, you can't.

KAI: You can't think sinking cruise ships is going to go unnoticed.

STEVE: Unnoticed? I'm kinda banking on it being noticed, Kai. What's it called? Collective action? *Good trouble.*

DELMAR: How on earth is this good???

STEVE, *pointing to his shirt*: Like the man says: EAT. THE. RICH.

DELMAR: What?!?

STEVE: The Russian Oligarchs. The Broligarchy. Literally, any billionaire.

DELMAR: People on cruise ships are hardly billionaires.

KAI: And, besides, that's not what the phrase means.

STEVE: Rousseau said, *"Quand les pauvres n'auront plus rien à manger, ils mangeront les riches!"*

DELMAR: *What.*

STEVE: "When the people have nothing more to eat, they will eat the rich!"

KAI: He didn't mean we should literally eat the rich.

STEVE: Yeah, but we could. And maybe we should! What's the carbon footprint of a single yacht owner? Eat an oligarch, save the planet!

DELMAR: Steve – what the fuck.

STEVE: They're ruining our hunting grounds! They're poisoning our waters! And all that noise their engines make? We should eat them just for that!

KAI: Steve, I agree. But I don't see how sinking their yachts will do anything to stop that.

STEVE: They feel some pain so that they can feel our pain!

DELMAR: That's not the way it works! They feel pain and then – they make us feel more pain.

STEVE: They'll be afraid of us sinking their boats, and they'll stay out of our waters!

KAI: Also not the way it works. They think of all waters as their waters.

STEVE: Even international waters?

KAI: Whatever. The point is, they don't think the waters are ours.

DELMAR: Will never be ours.

STEVE: And all that doesn't make you want to ram a yacht or two?

KAI: Ok. Steve. I understand how it would feel good, in the short term, to ram all the boats – but that's not action, that's anarchy!

STEVE: If anarchy means I get to ram more boats, then I want anarchy!

DELMAR: Steve, be serious. What, exactly, is your end goal?

STEVE: To make them realize that their actions have consequences! To make it clear we will not take their ongoing destruction of our environment without a clear and measured response!

KAI: You won't get that by sinking all the yachts!

STEVE: What about cruise ships? It's ok to ram cruise ships, right?

DELMAR: No, cruise ships are not ok! No sinking of any ships!

KAI: And as delicious as it sounds, eating billionaires won't solve the larger problem.

STEVE: We have to do something! We have to stand up to them!

DELMAR: Yes, they've created a big problem – but they're powerful!

STEVE: But... there are more orcas than billionaires.

KAI, *light bulb moment!:* ... There are *way* more orcas than billionaires.

STEVE: You're with me, right? What if we didn't sink the ships? What if we... circled them? You know, slowed their roll. And when they dump garbage, we just ram them a little.

DELMAR: Kai. You're not encouraging this, are you?

KAI: He's right, Delmar! We band together! But we need better t-shirts. Something like... "Your current pleasure is our future pain so please stop polluting our waters."

DELMAR: That's a terrible t-shirt. Plus, the print would be too small for anyone to read it.

STEVE: How about... "The Future Starts Now?"

KAI: Yes! "The Future Starts Now!"

STEVE: And it starts by eating the rich!

DELMAR sighs.

◊ ◊ ◊

Tira Palmquist is based in Southern California. She is known for plays that merge the personal, the political, and the poetic, such as *Two Degrees*, which premiered at the Denver Center and is available through TRW Plays. Her newest play, *The Body's Midnight*, premiered at Boston Court Pasadena in April 2024 (a co-production with IAMA Theater Company). Tira's current projects include *Memory of Winter*, a play continuing her series of plays about Minnesota, also about climate change, and *King Margaret*, an adaptation of the Henry VI cycle that was

featured in the 5 Directors, 5 Plays reading series with Oregon Shakespeare Festival in July 2021.
www.tirapalmquist.com

THE PRESENTATION

Juan C. Sanchez

The intention for this piece is to remind us to stay connected to the present moment and to embrace the promise of a new beginning. It's about accepting where you are – and where someone else might be – without judgment, holding space for honesty, compassion, and the quiet strength that comes from genuine presence.

Characters

LENA: Any age, ethnicity.
MARCOS: Any age, ethnicity.

Note

I've assigned genders to the characters, but they are not fixed. The roles can be played by actors of any gender.

◊ ◊ ◊

A backyard. The sound of a party inside. MARCOS looks into the distance with a drink in hand. After a few beats, LENA enters, also with a drink. She sees his back, looks where he's looking, and then approaches him, friendly.

LENA: Are you Susan's friend?

MARCOS: Oh! *(turns to face LENA)* Um, yeah… yeah, we've known each other since elementary school.

LENA: Wow, that's –

MARCOS: – a long time, I know.

LENA, *raises her glass*: Well, here's to friendship. The long-lasting kind.

They clink glasses.

LENA: She's been doing amazing work with climate change. No one rallies up people like she does.

MARCOS: She cares. About the planet. About people.

LENA: Profoundly. She's one of the good ones. Oh, by the way, I'm also a friend of Susan's. My name's –

MARCOS: We've met before.

LENA: We have?

MARCOS: Two years ago. The Climate Expo in Miami.

LENA: Oh, that was –

MARCOS: – a long time ago, I know. And we didn't really talk or anything. So it's not like we really met. But I went to your talk, the one about –

LENA: "Advocacy for Beginners."

MARCOS: Yeah, that one.

Beat.

LENA: And?

Beat.

MARCOS: It confused me.

LENA, *shocked*: Really? What confused you about it?

MARCOS: You know what? It doesn't really matter. And now that I think about it, it could've just been me… at the time… you know? Maybe my head wasn't, like maybe I wasn't –

LENA, *gently*: Hey… it's ok. You can tell me.

MARCOS: I'm sorry, it's just –

LENA: No, there's no need to apologize.

MARCOS: But –

LENA: Really, it's ok.

MARCOS: It made me angry. So fucking angry.

LENA: The presentation?

MARCOS: Yeah, this one section. One part of it.

LENA: Well, I wasn't expecting that. I mean…

Beat.

MARCOS: I'm sorry.

LENA: Don't be. But if there's anything you want to share. So I can address it, well… that would mean a lot to me. *(beat)* I'm not perfect, you know? Neither are you. Not even Susan, with her glorious, climate-crusader heart. But we can help each other. Guide, teach, call out each other when necessary. Even hold one another when the time calls for it. So if I failed in –

MARCOS: No, it's not that – it's… actually, I'm ok now. It's nothing.

LENA: Are you sure?

MARCOS: I'm good. Thank you. You're great. Like Susan. What you do, it's… well, thank you for doing it. For the planet. For us.

LENA: For me, too. I do it for myself. For clean air and temperatures that are – It's what I'm called to, I guess. But we're in it together, aren't we?

MARCOS: Yeah. *(beat)* I should, uh, get another drink, um… ok… bye.

MARCOS walks away but stops and turns.

MARCOS: That section of your presentation. After the guided meditation. When you asked us to recall a childhood moment of connection to nature –

LENA: Yes?

MARCOS: You took me there. I went back to when I was four years old. Sitting on my mom's lap on these huge, wet rocks by a waterfall. And she's holding me tight. Our legs stretched out into the water, warm and clear, slapping against our thighs. Me asking dumb questions: "Why are the rocks so slippery?" "Because they're wet," she said. "Why are you holding me so tight?" "Because I don't want the current to take you away." And I felt so loved. So protected. I'd look up at the sky and say, "I love the sky." I'd look at the water and say, "Mommy, I love the water." And the rocks. "I love the rocks. And you, mommy, I love you." So I'm in this moment, probably my first conscious connection to nature and how intertwined it was with loving and being loved… and the tears come. An unstoppable, endless stream of tears. Like a water faucet left running. And I tried to stop. I really did. I tried to will myself to stop, but I couldn't. Because I was also paralyzed. Like I had no access to my physical body, like I couldn't move. And that's when you ended the meditation and said, "This is when people become performative about their care, concern, and connection to climate change. This is the time for crocodile tears."

LENA: Oh my god, I –

MARCOS: I wanted to scream that I wasn't crying for the planet, carbon emissions, rising sea levels, or heatwaves.

LENA: I am so sorry, I –

MARCOS: I was crying for my mom. For that memory. For the love I felt.

LENA: That love and connection –

MARCOS: For months, I only thought of myself as the clown who cried fake tears.

LENA: Clearly, they weren't fake, they –

MARCOS: Then I started to think that maybe I didn't really care about the dying coral, the melting glaciers, or the Everglades. That maybe I wasn't built for any kind of advocacy.

LENA: What I said at that presentation had nothing to do with the beautiful memory that came to you. What you felt in that moment – that love, that connection – that's the point of it all. I'm sorry that our wires got crossed. And as far as advocacy goes –

MARCOS: I have these lemon trees on my balcony. They're half-dead now because I can't bring myself to water them anymore. I try, but then I think: What's the point? Everything feels so thick. Like the air's thicker and heavier. Like everything's –

LENA: Then stop thinking about everything. Think about one thing. Something small. Something you can touch.

MARCOS: Like what?

LENA: Like the lemon trees on your balcony.

MARCOS: But they're half-dead, remember?

LENA: Then water them.

MARCOS: Again, what's the point?

LENA: Take a moment. Stand back. Try to understand that you can't fix the planet all by yourself. Give yourself grace. Kindness. Know that there are things you can do – and should do – but the heavy lifting, we need to do together. And please, water your trees. Because they're still alive. And you can help them stay that way. And maybe if your trees don't die, the bees come back. And if the bees come back, they pollinate the bougainvillea. And maybe that tiny act of care ripples out in ways we can't see. And maybe, for you, for right now, that's all that's needed.

MARCOS breathes, lowering his head.

Juan C. Sanchez is a Cuban-born, Miami-based playwright dedicated to writing stories that explore the cultural diversity and social issues of Miami. He has written plays for a variety of platforms – from traditional theatre stages to immersive, site-specific performances set in historical motels, virtual stages, climate-change themed productions, and radio plays. Plays include the immersive *Miami Motel Stories* series, *Long Distance Affair*, *Versace Era*, *A Grey Divide*, *Paradise Motel*, and others.

ECO-ABORTION

Darrah Teitel

Since having kids, my only prayer has become: "May they be spared from the pain and grief of climate catastrophe." Perhaps the most fraught and growing conflict between ecological and human interests is reproductive: the choice to birth kids into these planetary death throes. I've worked hard as a reproductive and sexual rights activist and firmly believe that the choice to become a parent is an essential part of human self-actualization. Likewise, for those who don't want kids, having a baby can be self-obliterating. Perhaps this is why my darkest imaginings around climate change evoke a kind of suicide pact that humans are creating for themselves and the future. The question of why we would ever bring children into that pact is what I'm pursuing in this short play.

Note

Nihilistic as the content may be, I ask that it be played for max humor. The character of EMMA is meant to be ridiculous.

◊ ◊ ◊

A cozy office in an abortion clinic. It's a slightly shabby room with a wooden desk and folding chair for guests. If the set permits, hang a feminist poster on the wall. EMMA is seventeen, dressed in comfortable pink sweats and holding her phone. JOYCE is in her forties or fifties, dressed in jeans and a button down shirt. She's holding EMMA's medical chart, on which she takes notes in certain fields as the interview progresses. If possible, what EMMA is filming on her phone should be projected somewhere in the theatre, but if tech is not available, this is not essential.

EMMA: Ok, are you ready?

JOYCE: Sure. Yes.

EMMA: And see? Your face is totally blurred out. It's this really chill app that blurs out the faces and, wait – What do you want for voice distortion? Want to sound like a pimp crime boss or like Mickey Mouse sort of coked out chipmunk shit, or like a… a… Wait, there are some good ones here. Here – Say something real quick.

JOYCE: Testing. Hello. Testing. Hi, my name is Joyce. Oh, don't use my real name.

EMMA: Lolz! Of course not, Joyce. I'm gonna call you Margaret Atwood. Oh my god, tell me you've watched *Handmaid's Tale.* It's so good. Ok. Rad. Listen. This one's called female deep throat. *(She plays back the recording with the blurred face.)* Oh weird, I thought it would sound more, like, porny? Like someone deep throating and talking at the same time, but what do you think?

JOYCE: They probably meant the Watergate Deep Throat.

EMMA: Ohhh! Like underwater? How is that fair to deep throat underwater?! Hell, no!

JOYCE: Ok, Emma, we have to start. Are you ready?

EMMA: Ya, yup. Hang on. Ok. *(to her fans)* Hiiiiii everyone! So here I am in the abortion clinic, and I just want to give a huge shout out to you, my fans who are watching and my mom who's outside and watching this live – Hi Mom! I love you so much! – and to the awesome tight team at the abortion clinic reception who were, like, so sweet and chill. Seriously, you guys, they gave me high fives and let me pet their little dog, and they didn't want me to film them which is, like, totally understandable because, oh my god, do you know how many effing death threats these rad bitches get all the time? Like every day. Well, maybe not every day. I dunno. Margaret? *(cups her hands around her mouth and whispers as an aside)* Not her real name. *(back to normal)* Margaret, do you know how many death threats you rad bitches get every day?

JOYCE: Oh, umm… I don't know…

EMMA: Anyhow… So – Love to my whole community. *(blows kisses)* Honestly, the antinatalism folks and the deep ecologists and all my ecofeminist sisters, you're all so strong and so badass and I'm really excited to share this moment with you. Ok, so – I'm Emma Starling – *(cups her hands again and shoves her face close to the camera)* yes, my real name – and this is my abortion! Yayyy. I'm actually really excited. For the next three to ten minutes, you will get to witness the first live streamed eco-abortion pre-interview or, like, meeting with the doctor or whatever the heck you call it!

Beat.

JOYCE: Oh. Oh, it's me now? Ok. *(has a hard time not looking directly at the camera)* So, Emma, hi. How are you feeling?

EMMA: So excited. *(turns the camera around to herself again and speaks in a whisper)* That's Margaret. She's my doctor, and she's awesome and she's given us permission to film her because she supports the cause.

JOYCE: Sorry, Emma, I'm just – Sorry, that's not exactly true. Hi everyone. No, I didn't say that I support Emma's cause. I mean, I care about the environment, but what I said, just to be clear, is that I support Emma's choice to experience and discuss her abortion any way she chooses. I support her autonomy and her right to make this… uh… documentary.

EMMA: And that is *so* cool of you. Honestly, I feel like you're my mother.

JOYCE: Ok. Um… I'm just going to… *(looks back to her chart)* So, just to be clear, you've come here to terminate your pregnancy, which is seven weeks along, and you've heard your options and you've chosen to use a medical abortion, which you'll take orally or vaginally, in pill form. Two pills. That's what you chose before arriving here today?

EMMA: Yeah, so I thought about it a lot and I really want to support all the hard work my sisters did to make sure that I could get this medical abortion pill and I wanted to like give them my business, so yeah, I'm gonna do the pill, which is called Mifegymiso, that's Mife-Guy-Miso. Look it up. It's awesome.

JOYCE: Sorry, do you mean that you're choosing a medical abortion because of… politics?

EMMA: Yeah! Because, like, access to the pill was soo hard to get and it was such a big campaign, and we won! Shout out to all of you who worked so hard and so long. Congrats!

JOYCE: You won't support access to the medication politically by taking it. You can have a surgical abortion if you want, Emma.

EMMA: Oh, that's ok. I don't want.

JOYCE: Ok. So… um… How are you feeling about your choice to terminate your pregnancy today?

EMMA: Really good. Can I tell you why? *(directly to her fans in a compelling campaign voice)* We haven't done nearly enough to make this world safe for kids and until our climate-denying leaders in our corporate-controlled government start paying attention, we have to take a stand, as women, and protect little children from the future.

JOYCE: Ok, sounds good. Emma, can you look at me as we continue? Do you have someone here who can –

EMMA: All children are born into suffering and I hate suffering!

JOYCE: Sure.

EMMA: Don't you?

JOYCE: I mean… I do suffer… We all –

EMMA: And do you hate causing pain? I hate it when I hurt anyone. Even a little.

JOYCE: Of course, I try and avoid hurting people.

EMMA: I can tell, Margaret. You're, like, a super-compassionate person and a doctor and I don't know if you know this, but you – You're a healer.

JOYCE: Yes, I believe I do heal –

EMMA: No! No, Doctor Maggie! No, you're healing the future. Floods? Fires? Famine? Disease? War? Starvation? You are healing us all. You are healing *him*!

EMMA grabs JOYCE's hand and presses it to her lower abdomen.

JOYCE: Him…

EMMA: Yes… Can't you picture him? I had this dream… I'm a Scorpio? So, my dreams are always, like, full prophesies. So, I saw him. He was, like, perfect curly hair and beautiful blue eyes – but like that milky baby blue that you know won't stay blue and, oh my god, I loved him so much and I knew I should save him. I named him Richy.

JOYCE: Sometimes the increased hormones of early pregnancy can give vivid dreams and nightmares. When did you have this dream?

EMMA: Five months ago.

JOYCE: But you're seven weeks pregnant.

EMMA: I know, right? I feel like we're having a moment here. I think what we're doing here is really, really profound and just, like, meaningful. *(turns to her fans)* You guys, Maggie and I are having a moment. Look at her face. *(thrusts the camera in her face)* Oh, oops! It's all blurry for you, I'm so sorry fanny fans! I forgot!

JOYCE: I'm sorry. That makes me a bit uncomfortable.

EMMA: It's ok, they can't see you.

JOYCE: No, I know. I do have to get through these questions though.

EMMA: Yes! It's all you, babe.

JOYCE: Do you understand what's about to happen in your body and what you can expect in the next forty-eight hours? After you take the first pill, you will –

EMMA: By the time I take this first pill, more than two hundred thousand of my besties out in the community will have seen this video. The word eco-abortion will have been googled approximately two million times. By the time all the cramping and blood is over – *(to the camera)* yuck, by the way – *(turns it back to JOYCE)* what we did here will be on Substack and Reddit and YouTube and in about five days, when the abortion part is long over, the *New York Times* is going to interview me. Or maybe *Vogue*. Maybe both? Maybe they'll want to talk to both of us, Maggie. What do you think?

JOYCE: No, that's not what I do.

EMMA: Why?

JOYCE: I'm very uncomfortable with this, actually.

EMMA: Oh noooo… I'm so sorry!

JOYCE: Did you conceive this baby intentionally? Just so that you could –

EMMA: Baby? Did you actually say "baby?"

JOYCE: Pregnancy.

EMMA: Dude, I got the abortion doctor to call it a baby.

JOYCE: *Pregnancy* –

EMMA: I call him Richy. And yeah. Yes.

JOYCE: I see.

EMMA: Are those the pills? Like, there on the desk?

JOYCE: Yeah.

EMMA: Are you going to give them to me?

JOYCE, *breathing deeply:* Yes. Of course, I am.

EMMA: Great. *(takes them)* You know, you should consider changing the color.

JOYCE: Excuse me?

EMMA: Of the pill. Make it black. A beautiful black pill. Um, Joyce?

JOYCE: What?

EMMA: Are you going to give me that water glass? You want me to take the first one now, right?

JOYCE: Right. Sorry.

EMMA: Don't worry, babe. You're doing great. *(She swallows the pill and comforts JOYCE by patting her shoulder or leg.)* You did so great.

◊ ◊ ◊

Darrah Teitel is a playwright and socialist living in Toronto, where she currently works as a labor organizer. She is a graduate of The National Theatre School of Canada's Playwriting program. Her most recent credits include *Forever Young* (Great Canadian Theatre Company, 2022), *The Omnibus Bill* (Counterpoint Players, 2019), *Behaviour* (Great Canadian Theatre Company/ SpiderWebShow, 2019), *Corpus* (Teesri Duniya and Counterpoint Players, 2014), and *The Apology* (Alberta Theatre Projects, 2013). Darrah formerly worked for Action Canada for Sexual Health and Rights, where she is proud to have helped win numerous national campaigns that supported access to abortion.

WE'RE RUNNING OUT OF CHAIRS

Kirby Vicente

This is a demonstration of time.

Games allow me to perceive the world in more tangible systems where there are players, game masters, and consequences to each action. The climate crisis is a tragic repercussion from this dangerous game that we're all subjected to. I think once we perceive how this game works, maybe we'll have a chance to rig it and possibly turn things around for the better.

Notes

This is just a normal game of musical chairs. The music plays and the players circle around the chairs clockwise. However, the game has to be played in exactly five minutes. You also have the choice to use your own music – preferably, I'd use Daft Punk's *One More Time* but it's up to you!

Here's the catch: The music should get faster after each chair is removed. This game is to be played by 12 players.

Facilitators should introduce the rules of the game:

- Twelve volunteers are needed to play the game. Others can freely watch the game as they please.
- This is a normal game of musical chairs. However, we'll add another rule. Players should take a seat when:
    - The music stops.
    - They hear the words "sit," "seat," or "sitting."
- Listen, listen, listen.
- Whoever wins will get a token. A certificate, a paper, or a sign that vaguely says "Congrats, you're the only person who

survived! What's next?" Something like that. Or you can come up with your own!

- Feel free to break the rules of the game to your liking!

◊ ◊ ◊

The game begins with a monologue.

FACILITATOR: One of the healthiest and the most sustainable ways to help save the environment is to walk. "Walking produces less noise, pollution, and emissions that can be harmful for the environment." Yada-yada, you can google the impacts of walking.

So let's play a game of musical chairs!

The music starts.

FACILITATOR: This way, we're strengthening our limbs and relying less on harmful emissions, minimizing our carbon footprints by adding more environment-friendly footprints. Even if the world is burning, we're helping it by... burning calories.

Remove chair number one. Continue playing the music. This time, it's faster.

FACILITATOR: But if the roads aren't made for walking, shouldn't we commute more? Maybe ride a bike? I don't know. Where we live, bikers often get endangered by angry mobs of car drivers. I mean, seriously, we're taking one-third of the road, and you have almost two-thirds of it.

Bikes scare me. Maybe it's fine to take a seat –

The music stops.

– and start commuting, yes? That's also sustainable by the way.

Remove chair number two. Eliminate a player and continue playing the music. The music plays once more but faster.

FACILITATOR: Yesterday, I was rushing to do my errands so I took a motorcycle taxi. That's still commuting! Anyways, I passed by the garbage truck that went to our house that morning and saw it dump all of the trash into this mountain of garbage. And let me tell you how that was just a waste of my time, carefully doing my triple Rs, segregating my trash, and all that. I should sit on this thought.

The music stops. Remove chair number three and eliminate a player. The music plays again, faster. At this point, the players can start running, you can encourage it.

FACILITATOR: So, I took my time and really sat on the thought.

Stop the music. Remove chair number four. Eliminate a player and play the music once more, faster. The facilitator should take a seat and grab a bite on their fast food burger.

FACILITATOR, *in between bites*: I remember enjoying a juicy bite of this *(name of the fast food burger)* burger and watching some YouTube video on the oldest burger ever. That one still looked the same as when it was bought in 1998. It scares me to think that this burger can possibly outlive me. You guys want to sit and enjoy this one?

The music stops. Remove a chair and a losing player. Play a faster version of the music.

FACILITATOR: That was some philosophical burger-talk. Since fast food is cheaper, I tend to eat more of it these days. Every day, it gets more expensive, you know? The healthiest choice burns up my wallet so fast. So we go cheap, and cheap often comes in small packages. Small packages eventually end up as mountains of garbage – but they last. Just like that very old burger I mentioned.

The music stops. Remove chair number six and a losing player. Play a faster version of the music.

FACILITATOR: But what about us? Will there come a time when the microplastics in our bodies outlive us? That's possible. Science says that infants born in the late nineties up to the two-thousands are born pre-polluted. Sit.

The music stops. Remove the seventh chair and the losing player. Play a faster version of the music.

FACILITATOR: That means they're as old as us. Remember that cheap small package? When it doesn't end up as trash, it finds a place in our body. The world is big enough to hold all of our garbage but when it starts piling up, it eventually finds a space inside of us. You can't outrun what's inside of you, right? We can sit –

As the music stops, remove the eighth chair and the losing player. Music plays faster and faster and faster…

FACILITATOR: – and talk about action plans. I believe in the impact of individual actions. But I also believe that we should look at the big picture, at the stuff beyond our control. Let me ask a question.

Stop. Remove a chair and a player. Play the music faster than ever before…

FACILITATOR: When you lose in this game, is it because you weren't fast enough, or because there are fewer chairs to begin with? This game of musical chairs can only be played when there aren't enough chairs. The only thing you can control is your ability to get a seat. You cannot control the number of chairs or when the music stops. So you're stuck in a game where the chairs are running out and you need to take a seat.

The music stops. Lose the tenth chair and the losing player. Music plays faster and faster and faster and faster and faster and faster…

FACILITATOR: Like our time and our place here on this planet, the chairs are running out. It's only a matter of time until only one chair is left. But… how did the chairs come to life? Obviously, there's a chair factory in charge of producing them. That means that, by logic, there are still a lot of chairs.

No more music. Take away the eleventh chair and the losing player. You know what to do with the music.

FACILITATOR: So are we really running out of chairs? That's the story the chair factory made up so we can keep playing their game. Except the factory has control over the chairs. The game won't work if everyone has their chair – that's exactly what they fear.

There are no more chairs.

FACILITATOR: Survival isn't supposed to be a game. Everyone deserves to have a place on this planet.

The music stops. The facilitator starts bringing the chairs back to their initial spots. They encourage everyone to do the same.

FACILITATOR: Individual actions can only do so much. As long as the chair factory continues to play this game of musical chairs, we'll keep running out of them. But it's not too late. The music will continue to play, the world will move on again, and we might just create a world where there's a chair for everyone to sit in – a world where everyone wins.

Everyone takes a seat.

◊ ◊ ◊

Kirby Vicente (they/them) is a performance-maker and storyteller with a stark fascination for participatory work and multi/anti-disciplinary research. Channeling the erratic, explosive, and inquisitive energy of play, their creative practice revolves around various creative disciplines, embracing their desire to become a multi-hyphenated artist and storyteller. Kirby is one of the pioneers of Jungle Gym Play Laboratory, a Manila-based playground for developing multi-arts performances and collective creations that explore the intersections of art, games, and social justice.

SNOWFLAKE'S SPECIAL

Kevin Matthew Wong

The inspiration: It seems kindness is in short supply today. What if the natural world was looking out for us more than we think? I often think it is.

This is a comedic monologue featuring a literal snowflake named Special, who is on a mini-quest to make humans smile. Special wants to try some new jokes on some humans they discover, but they don't have much time…

◊ ◊ ◊

(from off stage) Hello? Hello? Is anyone out there?

(making their way on stage) Oh my gosh… Oh my gosh! It's humans! Hello, people!

(aside) I'm so glad I'm not performing for moss or grass anymore…

Can you… Can you see me?

> *The performer waits until the audience confirms they can see them.*

WHAT?! You can!? AND YOU CAN HEAR ME TOO!?

It's been so long since I've performed for humans! I hope my English *(or local language)* is still good enough.

This is incredible! Wow! Ok!

Beat as the performer does some sort of quick on-stage warm up.

(with the tone of a smooth stand-up comedian) Well, I've just dropped in – from the sky – and it's great to be here tonight in… uhm… in…

(asking for help from an audience member) Excuse me, do you mind telling me where I am?

Oh yes, thank you, in *(Insert name of audience's answer, or ad lib a fun response. Maybe add a local joke.)*

My name is Special. I'm a snowflake. You may remember me from my work in blizzards, ice storms, and romantic winter evenings gone by. Remember those? Yes, that was me! They used to call me Special because each one of us snowflakes is different, unique. But now, they call me Special because it's getting harder and harder to see one of us… But tonight, for one night only, you're in for a treat. Welcome to Special the Snowflake's Comedy Special! *(The performer can hold for applause or ad lib, like, "Try saying that five times fast.")*

Directors may want to use sound effects here, like a drum hit, or some sort of acknowledging the wordplay.

Listen, I don't have much time before I melt and I've got some new material to try… Are you ready?

Here goes:
How did the refrigerator greet the snowflakes? Ice to meet you.
Didn't like that one, eh? Tough crowd.

How did the little girl know the snowman was angry?
He gave her the cold shoulder.

Why don't polar bears get cold feet? They're extinct! Just kidding, they do get cold feet. And also… They're extinct! But you knew that already, eh? Too soon?

Ok, wow, that did not go as well as I hoped.
I'm embarrassed. Honestly, I'm really under-rehearsed… I spent the past three years swirling in a series of typhoons…

(sigh, beat) Listen, I don't have much time before I melt… and they told me my set could only be five minutes and I've used three of them on shtick.

But, for real though, once I do go… Who knows when I might be a snowflake again? I might be a polluted pond next… or a catastrophic cloud… or stuck hanging out at the bottom of the ocean. I don't get to pick. And there are fewer and fewer opportunities to be frozen.

So, this time is special for me too…

I wanted to come find you tonight because I knew if I ever became a snowflake again, I would want to make people smile. You humans used to look up at us in wonder, in awe. We used to know each other well. When you spotted some of us, you might hold hands, or snuggle, or run and scream with joyful abandon like you hadn't done since you were littler humans. I miss that joy. Seems like there's less of it now. I've missed you all.

Honestly, I've never even been inside a comedy club or a theatre or anything like that before tonight. But I wanted to see people smile again and I thought… Maybe comedy could do it?

But maybe to make people smile… it's enough to just be me: Special.

Oh no – I feel my legs are beginning to liquefy now, so before I go… If we never see each other again: thank you.

I hope I made a bit of your life special. I wanted to do anything I could to make things better for you.
Please know you made my time special too.

The actor pretends their arms are melting now.

Ok… and there go my arms too.

Thank you. Good night. Good luck!

Ice to see you!

◊ ◊ ◊

Kevin Matthew Wong (he/him) is a Hakka Chinese-Canadian theatre artist who works as creator, producer, and video artist. Kevin is the Director of Producing at Toronto's Why Not Theatre and is the creator of the Dora Award-winning multidisciplinary *Benevolence* series about Hakka (客家) history. Kevin is interested in creating work about guesthood, cultural preservation, and human connection. Kevin has collaborated with companies across Canada, the UK, US, Spain, Germany, Korea, and Australia kevinmatthewwong.com

www.ingramcontent.com/pod-product-compliance
Lightning Source LLC
La Vergne TN
LVHW010941110826
845149LV00013B/2699

* 9 7 9 8 9 9 0 5 4 3 9 2 8 *